HEY, DADDY!

Animal Fathers and Their Babies

To my brother, Vasco,
who is a wonderful daddy and grandpop

—*M. B.*

For another unique father, my brother, Ray Higgins

—*H. B.*

Ω
Published by
PEACHTREE PUBLISHERS, LTD.
1700 Chattahoochee Avenue
Atlanta, Georgia 30318-2112

www.peachtree-online.com

Text © 2002 by Mary Batten
Illustrations © 2002 by Higgins Bond

Printed and bound in China
Illustrations painted in acrylic on cold press illustration board

Book design by Loraine M. Joyner
Composition by Melanie M. McMahon

10 9 8 7 6 5 4 3 2 1
First Edition

Library of Congress Cataloging-in-Publication Data
Batten, Mary.
 Hey, daddy! / written by Mary Batten ; illustrated by Higgins Bond.—
1st ed.
    p. cm.
Summary: Introduces the important roles that some animal fathers play in the development of their
offspring, with examples of specific kinds of birds, mammals, and other creatures that thrive under
a father's care.
 ISBN 1-56145-272-6
 1. Parental behavior in animals—Juvenile literature. [1. Parental behavior in animals.] I. Bond,
Higgins, ill. II. Title.
 QL762 .B38 2002
 591.56'3--dc21
                                        2002000182

HEY, DADDY!
Animal Fathers and Their Babies

Written

by

Mary

Batten

Illustrated

by

Higgins

Bond

PEACHTREE
ATLANTA

AN ANIMAL BABY'S LIFE begins with a mom and a dad. But both parents do not always take care of their baby. Some babies—such as fish, snakes, and insects—can swim or crawl away as soon as they hatch. They don't need parents to care for them, so the mom and dad leave after the eggs are laid.

Some animal babies can't survive on their own, and they need help from at least one parent. Usually the mom alone takes care of the kids. But in some animal species, the dad plays a very important role. He may help the mom, or he may watch over the babies by himself. Some animal daddies care for their families in quite remarkable ways.

Daddy songbirds have to work hard. The father and mother share equally the important job of taking care of their babies.

The daddy blue jay helps the mom build the nest of twigs, sticks, moss, and grasses. He brings food to her while she sits on the eggs and keeps them warm. When blue jay babies hatch, they are blind, naked, and helpless. They need both parents' care to survive. The father blue jay helps the mother feed them juicy insects and worms.

In about a month, the babies can fly, and they leave the nest. Before they are one year old, they will find mates, build nests, and have babies of their own.

The mallee fowl is an Australian bird. The daddy mallee fowl uses leaves, twigs, moss, and sand to build a nest that looks like a small volcano with an opening at the top. It takes several months to build the nest. The mother bird lays her eggs in the nest, then leaves. The daddy takes care of the eggs all by himself.

He works ten hours a day tending the nest to make sure his babies will hatch. He covers the opening in the nest to protect the eggs. To keep the eggs from getting too hot on warm days, he opens the nest mound to allow heat to escape. In chilly weather, he may open the mound at noon to let the sun warm the eggs. When the chicks hatch, they dig their way out of the nest. They already have feathers and are able to fly. The daddy has done a good job.

Daddy phalaropes are shorebirds that live in Alaska. The daddy phalarope builds the nest. After the mom lays the eggs, the dad sits on them until they hatch. The female may mate with other males and lay several clutches of eggs. Then she returns to the sea.

The daddy takes care of the chicks by himself. He keeps them warm, leads them to a nearby pond for food, and warns them if enemies are close by. Young phalaropes are not as helpless as baby songbirds. A day after hatching, they can begin feeding themselves. Then some dads leave, but others stay with the chicks for about three weeks, until they can fly.

Emperor penguins live in Antarctica, the coldest place on Earth. Penguins are birds that have flippers instead of wings. They can swim but cannot fly.

After the female penguin lays an egg, she swims out to sea to eat and regain her strength. The daddy has an important job to do. He has to care for the egg. It's a tough job, but he's ready.

He has been eating a lot of fish, and he is very fat. He needs all that fat because he will not eat again for ninety days. During this time, he will lose half of his body weight, but he will not leave the egg until his chick hatches. The daddy penguin keeps the egg on top of his feet. The warm skin and feathers on his belly hang over the egg like a blanket and protect it from the icy cold. If he doesn't keep the egg warm, it will freeze. Several daddies usually huddle together, trying to stay warm in temperatures that can drop to 80 degrees below zero.

When the baby penguins hatch, their mothers come back from the sea. They are healthy and fat so they can feed their babies. The daddy penguins are very hungry and tired. Now it is their turn to swim out to sea and eat. Soon they will get fat again. Then they will return to help the mothers feed the hungry babies.

The Darwin's frog lives in the South American rainforest. This tiny frog daddy has an unusual way of caring for his young. He lets his babies grow inside the vocal sac in his throat. Normally, he uses his vocal sac like an amplifier to make his calls louder. The vocal sac can stretch into a large bag.

The mother frog lays twenty to thirty eggs on land, then leaves. The daddy guards the eggs for ten to twenty days. When the tadpoles are almost ready to hatch, he snaps them up with his tongue and slips them into his vocal sac, where they stay for about fifty-two days.

As the tadpoles grow and change into frogs, the daddy's vocal sac gets bigger and bigger. It gets so full he can't make a sound. It gets so full he can't even eat because he really has frogs in his throat!

When the babies are ready, they hop out of their daddy's mouth and into the world.

Most insects don't need a daddy or a mother to care for them. But there are a few exceptions.

The giant waterbug lives in ponds and rivers. The mother bug lays her sticky eggs on the daddy's back. He may have one hundred or more eggs stuck to his back at one time. He keeps them there for at least twenty days, staying near the water's surface so the eggs can get air. When the babies hatch, they stay on the daddy's back for only a few minutes. Then they swim away on their own.

The daddy seahorse is one of the most unusual fathers in the animal kingdom. Instead of the mom, it's the dad that gives birth! The mother lays her eggs in a special pouch in the daddy's abdomen. The eggs hatch inside the pouch, and the baby seahorses stay there until they grow strong. When they are big enough to take care of themselves, they pop out of their daddy's pouch and swim away.

Mice are mammals.
Mammal mothers give birth to live
young, and the mother nurses the babies.
In most mammal species, the mom cares for the newborns
by herself. But some mammal daddies, like the California mouse, share
the work with the moms. The daddy mouse helps take care of the babies from the
day they are born until they stop nursing when they're about five weeks old.
Mice babies grow up very fast. By the time a female mouse is eleven
weeks old, she can have babies. Male mice can become
daddies when they're a little older.

Beavers live in North America near streams and ponds. They use their sharp teeth for cutting down small trees to build large dens. These mammals mate for life and may live ten to fifteen years. Each year they have four to six babies.

Although beaver babies can swim the day after they're born, they are not ready to be on their own. Together the daddy and mommy beavers feed and protect their large family. The older brothers and sisters help, too. Young beavers stay with their parents for two years. Then they go off to mate and start their own families.

Baboons are primates, the group of mammals that includes monkeys, apes, and people. When primate babies are born, they can't do anything for themselves. They need so much attention that the mother often can't take care of them by herself. She needs help from the dad or from another adult.

The daddy baboon in East Africa baby-sits while the mother goes to find food. He carries the baby and protects it from enemies. Sometimes a male baboon will even adopt an orphan baby and take care of it.

Japanese macaque monkeys, also called snow monkeys, live in the highlands and mountains of Japan, farther north than any other nonhuman primate. The daddy macaque shares the parenting duties equally with the mom. He carries the babies and protects them from enemies. The daddy also helps to groom his young offspring by looking through their hair and picking off the pests that could cause itching and disease.

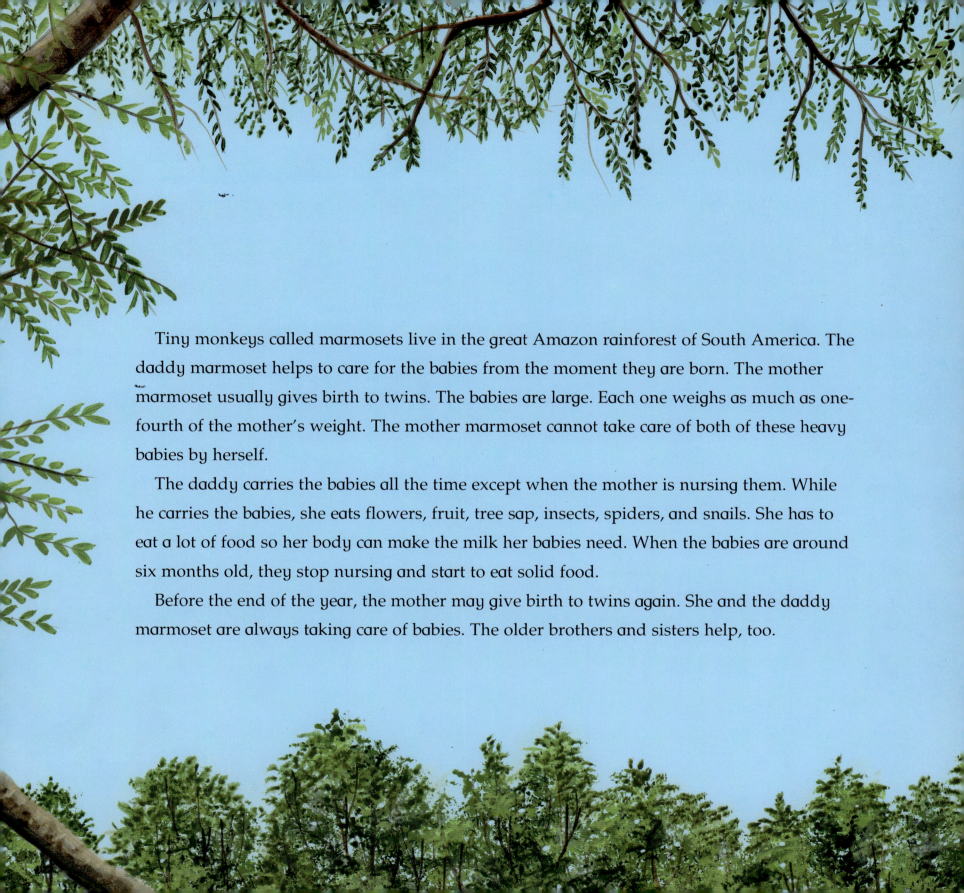

Tiny monkeys called marmosets live in the great Amazon rainforest of South America. The daddy marmoset helps to care for the babies from the moment they are born. The mother marmoset usually gives birth to twins. The babies are large. Each one weighs as much as one-fourth of the mother's weight. The mother marmoset cannot take care of both of these heavy babies by herself.

The daddy carries the babies all the time except when the mother is nursing them. While he carries the babies, she eats flowers, fruit, tree sap, insects, spiders, and snails. She has to eat a lot of food so her body can make the milk her babies need. When the babies are around six months old, they stop nursing and start to eat solid food.

Before the end of the year, the mother may give birth to twins again. She and the daddy marmoset are always taking care of babies. The older brothers and sisters help, too.

Mother and father titi monkeys stay together for life. They sit side by side on a branch in their leafy treetop home in the Amazon rainforest. They hold tails the way people hold hands. Every morning they call loudly to announce their home territory. After a baby is born, the daddy carries it most of the time. When it rains, the daddy shelters the baby. When the baby is hungry, he gives it to the mother to nurse. When the baby's tummy is full of good monkey milk, the mother gives the baby back to the daddy. Titi young stay with their family until they are about three years old.

The biggest daddy primate of all is the mountain gorilla of central Africa. The female mountain gorilla gives birth to one baby every three or four years. The big, fierce-looking silverback gorilla dad is the leader of his family. He is a peaceful animal unless his family is threatened. The silverback guards the females and babies and protects them from enemies. Sometimes he baby-sits while the females search for food. By the time young gorillas are two years old, they can travel on their own.

Seahorses, birds, and monkeys grow up much faster than we humans do. Baby seahorses are able to swim away and look after themselves right after they are born. Baby birds fly away as soon as their wings are strong. Monkeys learn to find their own food before they are one year old. Human babies need more care than any other baby animal, and they have the longest childhood of any animal. They aren't ready to live on their own for many years. Being a human mother or daddy takes a lot of work and a lot of love.

Human daddies are unique. They spend more time with their children than any other animal daddy. They love their babies, carry them, play with them, feed them, protect them, and teach them.

It takes someone very special to be a good daddy.